Charl

SCHOOL OF
Self-Defense

Charles Nelson's
SCHOOL OF
Self-Defense

The Red and Gray Manuals

CHARLES NELSON'S
SCHOOL OF
SELF-DEFENSE
151 West 72nd Street, New York 10023

Paladin Press • Boulder, Colorado

Charles Nelson's School of Self-Defense: The Red and Gray Manuals
by Charles Nelson

Copyright © 2007 by the estate of Charles Nelson
Foreword copyright © 2007 by Carl Cestari

ISBN 13: 978-1-58160-595-2
Printed in the United States of America

Published by Paladin Press, a division of
Paladin Enterprises, Inc.,
P.O. Box 1307
Boulder, Colorado 80306 USA
+1.303.443.7250

Direct inquiries and/or orders to the above address.

PALADIN, PALADIN PRESS, and the "horse head" design are
trademarks belonging to Paladin Enterprises and registered in United
States Patent and Trademark Office.

Visit our website at www.paladin-press.com.

Contents

Foreword

The innocuous sign on West 72nd Street announced "Charlie Nelson's School of Self Defense Combat Jujitsu and Karate." Bob Kasper and I climbed the stairs to the second floor and entered the studio apartment that served as Charlie's school. The walls were filled with magazine and newspaper clippings describing various real-world assaults and a plethora of martial arts and self-defense techniques. On one wall hung a mat and several heavy, canvas-stuffed mailbags. A dingy, time-worn carpet that had certainly seen better days covered the floor. The school was permeated with decades of Charlie's real-world experience in man-to-man violence. We scanned the school and saw a man of slight stature walking over to greet us. Frankly, I had a hard time believing that this individual could teach us anything about self-defense. I would soon, and painfully, learn otherwise.

After several minutes of "polite" amenities, we were anxious to get down to business and see just exactly what this man could really do. Charlie walked over to his desk, pulled tissues out of their box, and grabbed a knife. Approaching me from around the desk, Charlie tucked the wad of tissues in my shirt pocket and handed me the knife. Terse instructions followed: "Come at me with the knife."

I certainly didn't want to injure, or humiliate, this older gentleman, so I made a half-hearted approach with the blade. Charlie simply pushed me back and, shaking his head, said, "I told you to come at me—now come at me."

If Mr. Nelson wanted realism, realism he would get, I told myself, as I put a little more gusto into my assault. As I moved, Charlie spit right in my eyes, sidestepped, and kicked me square in the groin. He then kneed me in the face, hacked me on the back of the neck, trussed me in a bar hammer lock, and slammed me face first into that damn carpet. There I was held as Charlie explained that what he did, what he taught, was *real* street fighting. Charlie then rolled me over, took the tissues from my pocket, and wiped my eyes. I had a newfound respect for both Mr. Nelson and his system. It was an inauspicious beginning to a decades-long relationship.

That evening, on the train ride home, I read the stack of mimeographed information and letters on Charlie's methods. Anyone who ever met Charlie even once knew his proclivity for loading you up with all manner of paperwork, from historical copies to numerous personal letters, all praising his system and his teaching.

Charlie's personal background is an important key to understanding the Charles Nelson method. Raised as an orphan at a Catholic home for boys in upstate New York, Charlie was already developing those essential qualities of self-confidence and self-reliance at an early age. It was also at this orphanage that he was first introduced to the manly art of self-defense: boxing. This held him in good stead when, at age 19, he enlisted in the U.S. Marine Corps in 1934. It was here, in the Corps, that Charlie would discover his lifelong passion and calling.

While at Quantico as a member of the Marine boxing team, Charlie was introduced to the methods of Col. Anthony Drexel Biddle, who at the time was teaching FBI recruits at Quantico. As Charlie told the story, he met Colonel Biddle while returning from a remedial swimming course, since he had failed that part of basic training. Charlie stopped to watch Biddle instructing the FBI recruits in his particular form of man-to-man mayhem. Since the young Marine showed an interest, Biddle invited him to participate in the class. Charlie did so willingly. This was Charlie's first real exposure to a variety of armed and unarmed fighting methods. It would set the course for the rest of his life.

Charlie continued his training with Sgt. Patrick Kelly who had been with the Fourth Marines, also known as the "China" Marines. Kelly knew and trained under Dermot Michael O'Neil, who had served with the Shanghai Police and later as a close combat instructor under William Ewart Fairbairn for the OSS. Upon Fairbairn's recommendation, O'Neil had been seconded to the First Special Service Force, nicknamed the "Devil's Brigade." Charlie also was, for a brief time, a barracks mate of *Cold Steel* author and recognized close-combat pioneer, John Styers. Later in life, Charlie always gave credit to those who had influenced him in the development of his self-defense system.

In 1942, Charlie fought in the well-known battle for Guadalcanal with the First Marine Division. During this campaign, he was stricken with a severe case of malaria. In the throes of a high fever, virtually blind, with a battle raging all around him, Charlie resigned himself to an awful and bloody fate at the hands of the enemy. Thankfully, as the tide of battle turned in our favor, with the Marines brutally engaging the Japanese for every inch of blood-soaked territory, Charlie realized that he might very well, in fact, survive his ordeal. Soon after, he was evacuated and, after a time, recovered. This intimate encounter with his own mortality imbued in Charlie a certain attitude. Surviving the battle of Guadalcanal taught him to fear nothing.

Returning to New York City after the war with his wife, Alice, whom he had married before leaving for Guadalcanal, Charlie knocked around, trying to find his niche. It wasn't easy. He moved from one job to another, covering the gamut from short-order cook to doll salesman. The one constant was Charlie's pursuit of knowledge in the art of self-protection. After World War II, the country underwent many changes—most for the better, some for the worse. Violence and crime in urban America began to rise and catch the public's attention. Charlie realized that there was a realistic need for average citizens to be able to defend themselves against violent assault. He began what became a lifelong habit of scouring the daily New York papers and saving any articles about crime, violence, and self-defense. This study of assaults that had actually occurred would form the basis of his methods of personal protection. He continued to research and train in order to constantly update and refine his methods so that what he taught satisfied him as the most effective methods possible. The Nelson system drew on elements from diverse sources ranging from military combatives to tai chi chuan.

Charlie eventually set up his first "school of self-defense" in the living room of his apartment. As his reputation spread and his clientele grew, he moved to his first commercial location. His methods were direct, effective, and practical for average men, women, and even children. Even highly experienced and trained martial artists sought out Charlie for his realistic and practical teachings. Charlie credited Chinese guerrilla warfare as providing him with the foundation of his approach to self-defense, whose fundamental basis is the concept of withdrawal or retreat and immediate counterattack. This approach was epitomized in the logo of Charlie's school: the classic battle between the mongoose and the cobra. In this fight to the death, the mongoose draws out the cobra; then, as the cobra sees an opportunity and strikes, the mongoose deftly evades the strike and immediately counterattacks. The cobra, unable to recover from his missed opportunity, falls prey to the cunning counterassault. This principle is evident throughout Charlie's system of instruction.

From a technical perspective, Charlie's methods worked primarily because of deft footwork and concise body evasions. This is the real key, or secret, to the Nelson system. Charlie's uncanny ability to seemingly be one move ahead of his assailant rests almost solely on his ability to outmaneuver his attacker. The actual physical retaliation—consisting of blows, kicks, joint locks, and takedowns—works only when rooted strongly in properly executed footwork and evasive body mechanics.

Many, many individuals climbed those stairs to Charlie's school of self-defense. While most came with a sincere desire to learn effective and pragmatic tactics of personal defense, some came solely to test the "old" man. Charlie handled the latter as if he were playing with a small child. Invariably, the scenario unfolded this way: The joker would attack Charlie any way he wished and would suddenly, and painfully, find himself dispatched with a swift and smoothly executed counterattack. Picking himself up, Mr. Joker would say,

"Try that again and I'll show you what I do." The scenario would unfold again, except Charlie would execute a totally different defense. And, once again, the challenger would find himself face down, buried in that infamous, ancient carpet. The defeated assailant would protest that Charlie hadn't reacted the same way. Charlie would smile and remind the deflated know-it-all that a technique in the real world only had to work once. If Mr. Know-It-All had anything on the cap, he would realize what a gem he had found in Mr. Charles Nelson and become a devoted and humbled student.

Charlie's influence ran the gamut from professional law enforcement (city, state, and federal) to military personnel, celebrities, and those involved in the seamier aspects of personal conflict and "security." Many well-known martial artists sought out and studied Charlie's methods. These included the much beloved and respected Professor "Vee" Visitacion, Brad Steiner, Bob Kasper, Geoff Todd, Ralph Grasso, and many others too numerous to mention. Charlie's expertise was also recognized by the judicial system when he was called to testify as an expert witness in a homicide case involving the use of a "judo" choke.

The methods demonstrated in the two manuals reprinted in this book offer an accurate picture of the Nelson system. They are concise, pragmatic, and highly effective. They can be easily understood, practiced, retained, and executed under the worst conditions of actual violence. The volumes of letters written to Charlie by former pupils, expressing gratitude for teaching these life-saving tactics and methods, attest to the efficacy of the system.

Over the years, Charlie's training and methods changed and were adapted. At one time, his system stressed impact more than control and submission. Early on in his teaching career and as a younger man, Charlie was known for practicing on a full-sized tugboat bumper that was bolted to the wall of his school. He would also shock onlookers by randomly shattering pieces of concrete with various punches and strikes. But as Charlie got older, his methods changed accordingly. He shifted his focus to the use of more cunning and deception. The red and gray manuals are the culmination of decades of knowledge and experience and show a well-balanced and equally adaptable system by individuals of any stature, age, or gender.

Charlie Nelson with Carl Cestari.

Charlie Nelson was one of those rare individuals who are fortunate enough to live their passion. He truly epitomized the old cliché about forgetting more than most people know. Those of us who were lucky enough to have known, and trained under, Charlie benefited in many ways from that relationship. Hopefully, with the wider circulation of these manuals, thanks to Paladin Press, many more people will be lucky enough to attain some insight into this unique man and his life-saving methods.

—Carl Cestari
January 2007

Section I

Photographs

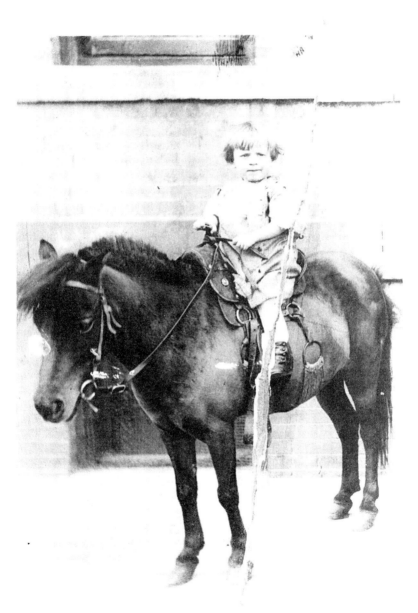

Charles Nelson, 3 years old, 1918.

Nelson in his full-dress Marine Corps uniform in the 1930s.

USMC Platoon Sergeant Charles Nelson, Camp Lejeune, North Carolina, c. 1936.

The School of Self Defense logo with the mongoose and the cobra. Nelson opened his first studio, School of Self-Defense, on 104th and Broadway in 1949. In 1955 or '56, the studio moved to West 79th between Amsterdan and Columbus. Then in 1959 Nelson moved the studio to West 72nd and changed the name to Charles Nelson's School of Self-Defense. The school remained at this location until Nelson retired in 1998 and moved to Arkansas.

SCHOOL OF SELF DEFENSE

CIVILIAN • POLICE • SECURITY
SELF DEFENSE · STREET FIGHTING
ANTI-MUGGING · ANTI-RAPE TECHNIQUES

CHARLES C. NELSON
FORMER INSTRUCTOR
U.S. MARINES
EST. SINCE 1946

151 W. 72ND ST
N.Y.C. 10023-3225
212-362-3896

Charlie Nelson's business card for his self-defense school on 72nd Street.

Charles Nelson's School of Self Defense, New York City.

The Nelson family in front of their apartment in New York City, 1955: Charles (40), Alice (33), Bryan (9), and Carol (3). Charlie taught in the family apartment before he rented a studio.

Rare photo of Nelson teaching jujitsu in his early 40s. He eventually gave up practicing in uniform and only worked in street clothes. One of his favorite sayings was "A black belt is only good to hold up your pants."

September 26, 1984

Mr. Charles Nelson
151 West 72 Street
New York, NY 10023

Dear Mr. Nelson:

As you know, on March 6, 1984, at about 1 PM, two men
attempted to rob me on the #1 IRT subway train northbound,
between the 18th street and 23rd street stations. One was armed
with a .25 caliber auto pistol; the other was armed with a large
knife. The man with the gun sat down next to me, on my left side;
the man with the knife sat down next to me on my right. The gunman
pointed his pistol straight at me, and told me that if I did not
"give it up", he would blow my head off. I told him "Okay, okay,
I'll get it," and reached into my righthand coat pocket for my
revolver. I was able to draw my gun from my coat pocket, deflect
the gunman's pistol arm, and shoot him. The second man fled the
subway car, but was captured later that same evening. He is now
serving a minimum of two years imprisonment. I credit your course
with greatly increasing my knowledge of disarming techniques, of
guns and knives both. It also improved my reflexes, but it helped
my thinking the most: more important than techniques, you teach
people practical attitudes. Often, it is better to appear to
submit before resisting: you stress this. All too sadly, many
a police officer (or other person) has been hurt by an overly
macho attitude that he or she must rush into a fight without
thinking first.

I know your course contributed materially to my survival,
and I want to thank you for that. I have recommended your course
to others, and would not hesitate to recommend it to anyone who
wants a good, basic, practical course in self defense. Once again,
thank you for your instruction.

                              Sincerely,

                              Adam Kasanof

A 1984 letter from a police officer who credited his training with Nelson for saving his life when he was attacked by two armed men on a subway train. This was
just one of many letters Nelson received from satisfied students.

WILLIAM A. JACKSON
333 GARDEN CITY ST.
ISLIP, TERRACE
NEW YORK, 11752
WINTER, 1986

MR. CHARLES NELSON
151 WEST 72ND ST.
NEW YORK, NEW YORK

MR. NELSON,
ON BEHALF OF MY BROTHER, JOSEPH,
AND MYSELF I WOULD LIKE TO TAKE THIS OPPORTUNITY TO THANK YOU
FOR PROVIDING US WITH THE BEST PRACTICAL POLICE TRAINING
AVAILABLE ANYWHERE.

BOTH OF US HAVE HAD EXTENSIVE BACKGROUNDS IN MARTIAL
ARTS AND WESTERN STYLE BOXING OVER THE YEARS. WE HAVE BOTH
BEEN THROUGH OUR RESPECTIVE POLICE ACADEMIES WITH ALL OF
THEIR DEFENSIVE TACTICS AND TO DATE NOTHING COMES CLOSE TO
YOUR METHODS FOR SIMPLICITY, EFFECTIVENESS AND TRANSITION OF
MOVEMENTS.

FORTUNATELY, WE BOTH WERE IN THE MARINES DURING THE
SIXTIES AND HAD AN INTRODUCTION TO YOUR BRAND OF COMBATIVES.
THIS MADE UNDERSTANDING AND LEARNING YOUR TECHNIQUES ALL THE
EASIER FOR US. YOU HAVE TAKEN ALL FORMERLY DEADLY JIU-JITSU
TYPE TRICKS AND MODIFIED THEM TO WHERE WE CAN APPLY THEM TO
UNRULY, DISRUPTIVE AND ASSAULTIVE PEOPLE ON THE STREETS. THIS
IS DONE WITH MINIMAL INJURY TO THE SUBJECT AND MAXIMAL
PROTECTION TO THE POLICE OFFICER.

THE MOST OUTSTANDING FEATURE ABOUT YOUR TEACHING IS THAT
IT IS DIRECTLY APPLICABLE TO ALL. NAMELY, LAW ENFORCEMENT,
MILITARY PERSONNEL, SECURITY PEOPLE, AND THE LAYMAN IN
GENERAL. THERE IS NO NEED FOR ANY PRIOR EXPERIENCE IN ANY
FORM OF SELF-DEFENSE. IN FACT, IT IS PROBABLY BETTER FOR
THOSE WHO HAVE NO OLD, BAD HABITS TO UNLEARN. YOU HAVE THE
INHERENT GIFT OF SEEING WHAT WORKS AND REFINING THE MOVES TO
THE EXTENT THAT ANYONE CAN LEARN TO ADEQUATELY DEFEND HIM/HER
SELF IN A SHORT PERIOD OF TIME WITHOUT ALL THE ORIENTAL
MYSTERY AND TRAINING COSTUMES WHICH PERMEATE TODAY'S MARKET.

BOTH JOE. AND I HAVE ALWAYS BEEN THOUGHT OF AS COMPETENT
ON AND OFF THE STREET. NOW, THANKS TO YOU, WE CAN FEEL AND
ACT THAT MUCH MORE CONFIDENT IN OUR EVERYDAY DEALINGS WITH
"STREET SLIME." WE BOTH KNOW THAT THE ONLY "BELT" OR TROPHY
OR "RANKING" THAT REALLY COUNTS IS BEING ABLE TO GO HOME
AFTER WORK IN THE SAME CONDITION WHICH WE STARTED.

TO WHOEVER READS THIS: TAKE HEED, THE LIFE YOU SAVE MAY
BE YOUR OWN!
SEMPER FI,
BILL JACKSON

Another letter (1986) thanking Nelson for the training the writer and his brother, both
police officers, received from Nelson. Both brothers believed that Nelson's training
far exceeded what they received at their respective police academies.

Charley's Lessons in Leverage.
First You Run

"THIS big guy, six-one, 200 pounds, grabs you in a choke hold," says Charley Nelson, a little guy, five-eight, 130 pounds, wrapping his fingers around my neck. "Whatcha gonna do?" Depends on the neighborhood, I want to say. I'll either call a cop or go up to the Bronx and buy a gun. But Charley has no sense of humor about such things, so I say, "Grab his right sleeve with my left hand, swing my right arm . . ."

"Yeah, yeah," says Charley, faintly disappointed. "That's what I taught you 35 years ago, but I refined it. I got a new move. Here, you choke me."

•

Charley Nelson daydreams urban nightmares. He is always refining a small move, the twist of a wrist, the angle of a hip, that will send a big guy, six-two, 220, crashing to the pavement, sorry he ever tried to rob or rape or kill you. Charley considers himself a body mechanic, looking for leverage in a city filled with even more bad big guys than when I first went to him at 19. In those days, he would never have thought about aggressive beggars; these days he shows me the two-handed punch for bums who get too close. But his philosophy has not changed.

"First," he says, "you want to avoid the problem, which means be alert. Don't walk around reading a book. Keep looking around out of the corner of your eyes. You don't want to make direct contact, challenge some punk, make some crazy think you're trying to penetrate his brain with laser rays."

The 5:30 P.M. class, consisting of a high school sophomore, a file clerk and a hotel doorman, drifts into the small, shabby loft on West 72d Street in Manhattan. There is an impromptu feel to Charley's pedagogia that reflects the streets more realistically than the martial-arts dojos that have become the ballroom-dance studios of paranoia.

"If you can't avoid the problem, try to run away," Charley continues. "That's no shame. Apologize, even if it wasn't your fault. Give up your wallet. Men seem better at that, maybe because they think they're stalling for time, looking for an opening. Women hang on to their pocketbooks like it was part of their body.

"If you got no choice, then you fight dirty. Popping out eyeballs is good. Kicking in the groin is too obvious unless you first feint popping out eyeballs. Head butt to the nose. Stomping real hard on an instep always works. Lots of little bones in your instep."

Robert Zimmerman

The three young men shuffle through plastic pistols, rubber knives, bats, reams of photocopied newspaper scare stories with headlines like "Fights for Life After Knifing." They kick and chop at patched mats and taped duffel bags hanging on a peeling wall. They work out in the clothes they are wearing; no mugger waits for you to put on your "Karate Kid" uniform, Charley sneers. No flips, no tumbling here; this is all mean little movements of elbows, knees, heels, a shark bite to the thigh of a sexual harasser.

Charley is 78, but he looked old and scuffed and easy to hit when he was 43 and told me, "Never kill a guy just for being clumsy," a liberating order from a self-defense teacher. I didn't have to be macho; I could finesse, excuse, grovel, turn tail. Coping in the streets is about getting out alive, not about finding your self-respect through some fool's fear.

Born in Bay Ridge, brought up in Catholic institutions and foster homes, Charley kept running away until he was old enough to join the Marines in 1934. He boxed and studied jujitsu. He was promoted to sergeant and became a hand-to-hand combat instructor. He was evacuated from Guadalcanal with malaria. Later, he became a toy salesman.

In the scene that has tantalized every actor and writer who ever took Charley's course, a big floorwalker, six-three, 240, threw him out of an East Side variety store and began stomping on his music boxes. Charley beat him up and opened his first studio.

He was ahead of the self-defense boom. Then he was overshadowed by what he calls "the Oriental mystique." The martial arts offer a guruism, a spirituality, that Charley dismisses. "Go to church," he growls. His students, many of whom are local and suburban police officers, pay $400 for 15 sessions that deal directly with their problems. The 26-year-old file clerk, Drew Hester, slim and reserved, says he wants "to feel less afraid." The doorman, 35-year-old Philip Ellis of the Waldorf-Astoria, a student for 12 years, shows Mr. Hester some simple ways to break free of a big guy who grabs your wrists. There will be time for the more intricate responses to someone with a gun at your back or a knife at your throat.

Sixteen-year-old Hugo Haneo has a problem that boxing lessons have not solved: the rough teen-agers at Martin Luther King High School over on Amsterdam Avenue. "Like in the halls, you always get a shoulder, an elbow," he says.

"Do it," Charley says.

It takes Mr. Haneo a moment to understand how serious Charley is. Then he swaggers into the little old man and throws a shoulder, which never connects. Charley's footwork is almost dainty as he pivots, and his hand movements are small, quick touches on the teen-ager's arm and back that slam him into a wall.

"Got to remember," Charley says, "a man's arm is like the tiller of a ship: you can steer him with it. C'mon." He signals to Mr. Haneo, whose eyes are shining with urban nightmares he will win. "Let's say a big guy, six-four, 250, grabs you from behind . . ."

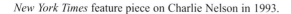

New York Times feature piece on Charlie Nelson in 1993.

Nelson offered his self-defense instruction to anyone who was interested, including women and children.

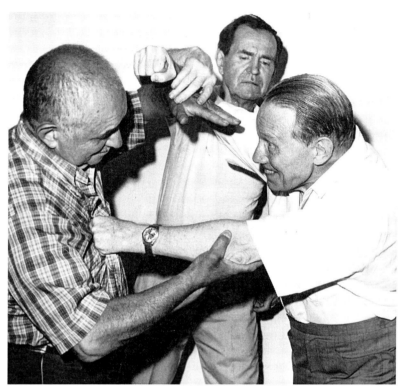

Nelson taught senior citizens once a week at no charge.

Nelson teaching his self-defense system to two students in his school, 1980s.

This photo from the late 1970s or early 1980s shows Nelson's famous cluttered desk.

Nelson receiving one of many awards. Behind him are the many news articles he liked to hang on the wall.

Charles Nelson in his studio.

Nelson with actor Robert Duvall in the 1980s. Nelson trained many celebrities, including cast members of several Broadway plays.

Nelson with certified instructors in his system (left to right): Geoff "Tank" Todd, Paul Gerasimczyk, and Herb Kantrowitz.

Charles Nelson, 73, with his wife, Alice, in 1988. They lived in this apartment above his studio.

Charles with his daughter, Carol, 1990s.

Charlie Nelson, 88, one month before his death in 2003.

Charles Nelson's gravesite in Jacksonville, Arkansas.

Close-up of the School of Self-Defense logo on Charles Nelson's headstone.

Close-up of the plaque honoring Nelson's service with the United States Marine Corps in World War II.

Section II
The Red Manual

Self-Defense

by

Charles Nelson

CHARLES NELSON'S
SCHOOL OF
SELF-DEFENSE
161 West 72nd Street, New York 10023   212-362-3996

Paul Gerasimczyk took the photographs of the techniques in this manual, and Allen Tino posed for the pictures with Charlie Nelson and wrote the captions.

**Charles Nelson's
School of Self-Defense
151 West 72nd Street
New York, NY 10023
(212) 362-3896**

I was born in the Bay Bridge section of Brooklyn. When I was three years old my parents separated, and I was placed in an orphanage under the care of Catholic nuns. When I was around eight, I was sent to a home run by Christian brothers, who taught me to play baseball and how to box. If we got into a fight, the brothers made me put on boxing gloves and settle it.

At the age of fourteen, I was placed on a farm in upstate New York. I ran away and lived on other farms. When I was nineteen, I joined the Marine Corps and served for ten and a half years. When I joined in 1934, the Marines were teaching hand-to-hand combat, bayonet fighting, and jiu-jitsu—all of which I absorbed. I trained with other Marines and F.B.I. agents under Colonel Biddle. I also met a Sergeant Kelly, who had been attached to the International Police in Shanghai, China, in the 30's. This is how I came to learn a unique fighting method that no one else in the U.S. teaches.

This method is based on Mongolian wrestling techniques intended to maim or cripple. Combined with other methods that I studied through the years, these techniques form a complete system. My method combines boxing, jiu-jitsu, karate, principles of Tai-Chi and Aikido, and dirty fighting. Keeping only what is useful and practical for self-defense, there is not a wasteful technique.

Over the years I have had many students with black belts in other martial arts come to me; all were amazed at how little they knew about real self-defense, despite years of training. They felt my method had rounded out their knowledge of self-defense.

Many black belts and other so-called experts in the martial arts have been killed or injured in street fights because their skills didn't work outside the dojo. I am convinced that anyone, even with no prior martial arts training or experience, can learn to defend themselves in any ordinary life-and-death situation.

Yours in Self Defense

Charles Nelson

Former Instructor, U.S. Marines

Lessons by Appointment Only

Attacker extends his left hand to push you backwards.

Defense: Take his left wrist with your right hand; step back on your left leg, turning to
your left and pulling him toward you. A right side-kick to his left knee will stop him.
To control him: Turn his left palm up, grab the back of his left hand with your left hand
(just above his knuckles), bend his wrist and bear down on his elbow. You can subdue
him or break his arm at the elbow joint.

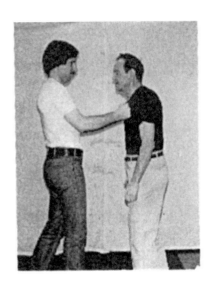 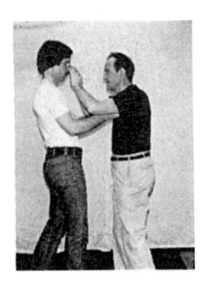

Attacker pulls you toward him, or out of a car, or up from a chair.

Defense: Move into him delivering finger jabs to the eyes. Thrust knee into his groin, driving upward.

Attacker grabs you with his left hand, his arm bent slightly, pulling you toward him, and he is threatening you with his right hand.

Defense: Lightly grabbing his left elbow with your right hand, side step diagonally forward to your right. At the same time, drive a left heel-palm thrust under his chin (snapping his head back) and thrust your left knee up into his groin.

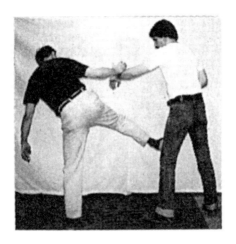

Attacker throws a straight left jab at your face.

Defense: If possible, step back on your left leg; deflect his left arm with your right by chopping at the wrist or forearm; deliver a right side-kick to his knee.

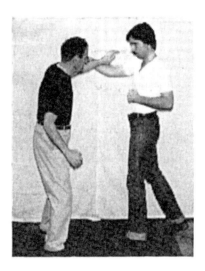

Attacker throws a right-hand punch.

Defense: Side-stepping to your right, block with your left hand inside his right arm and deliver a front snap-kick to his groin. Practice this side- step-block-kick until it becomes a fluid movement.

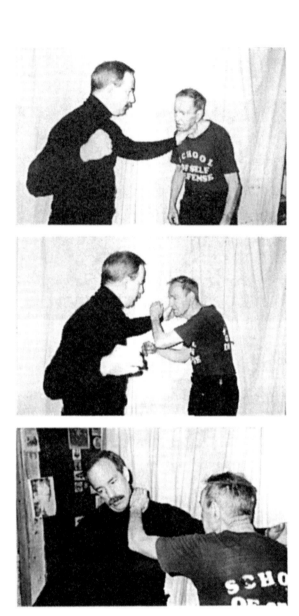

Attacker pins you against the wall by grabbing your throat with his left hand, and threatens you with his right.

Defense: With the palm of your left hand hit his left wrist out to your right side. This breaks his grip and cocks your arm for a knife-edge strike to the left side of his neck.

 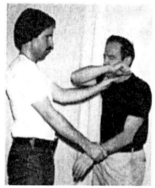

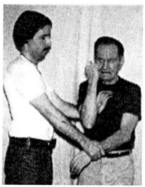

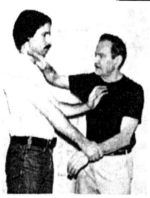 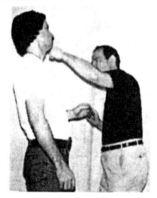

Attacker grabs you in a one-hand choke with his left hand and holds your left wrist with his right hand.

Defense: Turning, swing your right arm over his left arm (keeping your forearm horizontal), then snap downward as shown. Strike back with your right hand to the right side of his neck. Follow up.

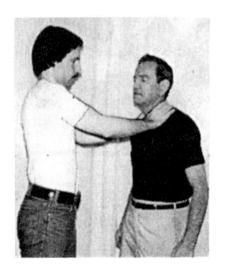 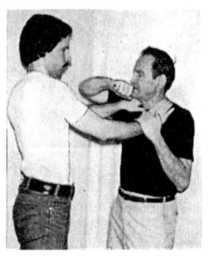

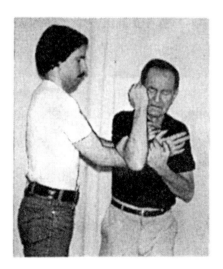

This time, attacker grabs you in a two-hand choke.

Defense: While pinning his right wrist with your left hand, step back on your left leg. Swing your right arm over his arms (with you forearm horizontal) and snap downward as shown. Strike back with a chop as you did with the one-hand choke.

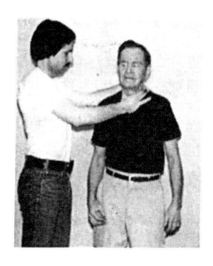 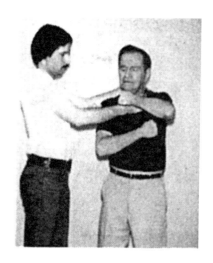

 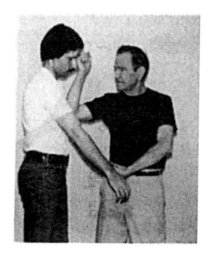

Attacker chokes you from the right side using two hands.

Defense: Grab his right thumb with your left hand while cocking your right arm. Simultaneously pull his right hand with your left and strike his solar plexus with your right elbow. Follow up with a back-fist to the face.

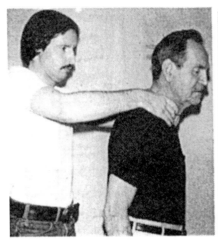 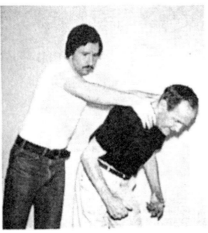

Attacker grabs you from behind in a two-hand choke.

Defense: Step forward on your left leg, bending forward at the waist to utilize your back muscles. Do not twist or you'll wring your neck. Back kick with your right leg (your foot will be in a side-kick position). When he lets go, drive a back fist into his groin.

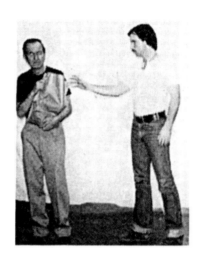 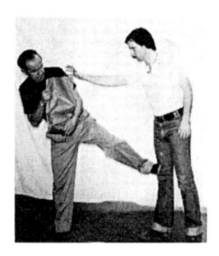

Attacker attempts to grab you while you are carrying a package.

Defense: Deliver a side-kick to his closest leg. Please note: the defense is the same whether he reaches with one hand or two.

Attacker attempts to grab you while you are carrying a package—this time you are facing him.

Defense: Throw the package in his face; immediately fire a front-kick to his groin. Attack him with chops to the throat or a palm-heel to the chin.

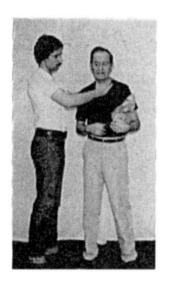 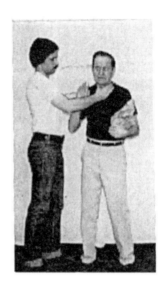

Attacker grabs you in a two-hand choke from your right side. You are carrying a package in your left hand.

Defense: With the palm or knife-edge of your free hand, hit his right wrist to your left side. Strike back with the point of your elbow to his solar plexus. Then a back-fist to his face or groin.

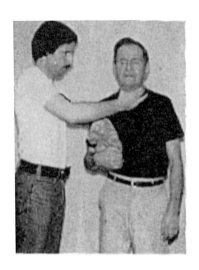

Attacker grabs you in a two-hand choke from your right side. This time you are carrying a package in your right hand.

Defense: With your left hand, grab his right thumb and pull it down and out to your left side. At the same time, scrape his shin with the edge of your right shoe and stomp on his instep. Step out to your right and deliver a left swivel-punch to his solar plexus.

 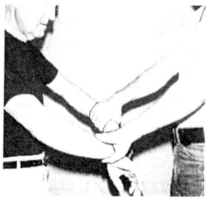

 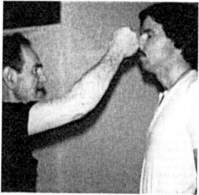

With your arms up in front of you (in what is sometimes called the "peaceful stance") an attacker grabs your wrists.

Defense: Stepping back on one foot, snap your wrists down against his thumbs and, in a circular motion, bring them outside of his arms and up together in front of your chest ready to deliver a double punch to the eyes or face.

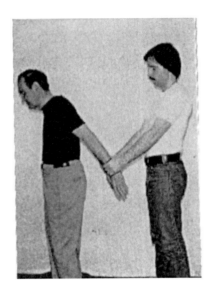 

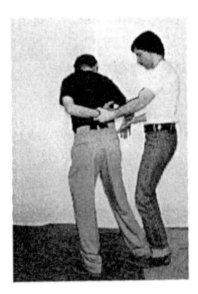

Attacker grabs both of your wrists from behind.

Defense: Step back on your left foot and twist to your right, letting your left arm bend up your back. Stomp high on his instep with your right foot. Follow up with a right elbow to the body and a back-fist to the face.

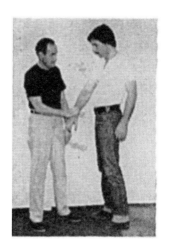 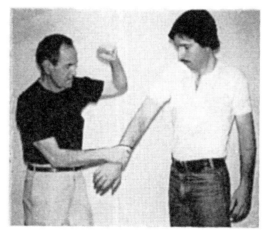

To get someone in an armbar.

From his right side grab his right wrist with your right hand as shown. Raise his arm up and to the side while turning his palm up. With the bony part of your left forearm (the ulna bone), hit the back of his arm at about the middle of the triceps muscle (this can paralyze his arm). At the same time pull him to your right side to get him off balance.

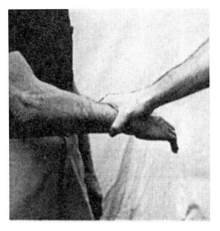
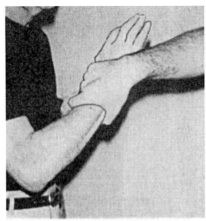

The Japanese double-armlock can be used either defensively or offensively. Here it is being used defensively against an attacker who grabs your right wrist with his right hand.

Defense: Using a circular motion, bring your right hand up at the angle shown and grab his right wrist. With your left hand, slap his nose, then reach over and under his right arm and grab your own right wrist. Apply pressure by twisting to your left, extending your left arm, and raising your right elbow. Bring your right knee upward into his groin.

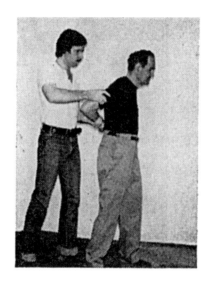 

Attacker holds your right arm in a hammerlock.

Defense: Step forward on your left foot with toes pointing to your right side (this will position you for the next move). As you pivot to face your opponent, snap your right arm down, then up toward your chest. Deliver a blow to his face or body with your left.

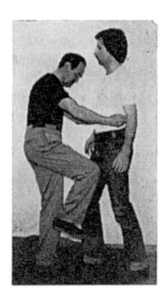

To prevent a front bear hug:

Spread both of your arms at the angle shown—this stops the attacker from completing his hold. Bang your forehead into his nose and drive your knee up into his groin.

.

Attacker catches you in a front bear hug—his arms under yours.

Defense: With you left hand holding the small of his back, strike under his chin or nose with the heel of your right hand - snapping his head back. Thrust knee into groin.

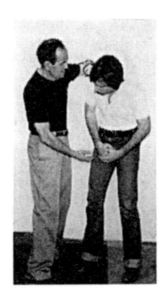

Attacker catches you in a front bear hug—his arms over yours.

Defense: Roughly grab his testicles; follow up with strikes and kicks.

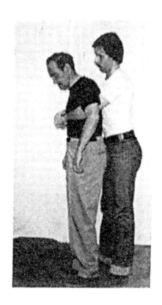

Attacker grabs you in a rear bear hug—his arms under yours.

Defense: Stomp on his instep: turning, deliver an elbow strike to his face or neck; drive the heel of your palm up into his chin.

Attacker attempts to get you in a full nelson.

Defense: Clamp down on both of his arms as shown in photo 2. Stomp on his foot, step out to your right side, hammer his groin with the bottom of your left fist, then strike his face with your left elbow; follow with a right palm-heel under his chin.

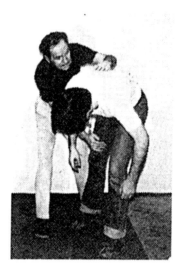 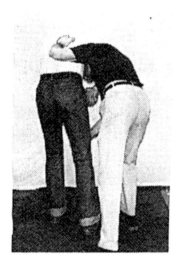

Attacker has you in a side headlock.

Defense: Using your outside hand (the right hand in this case), pinch the inside of his leg* while striking hard with the palm of your opposite hand between his shoulder blades. This will cause him to release his grip and stumble forward.

*This is the location of the femoral artery and nerve—a very tender area.

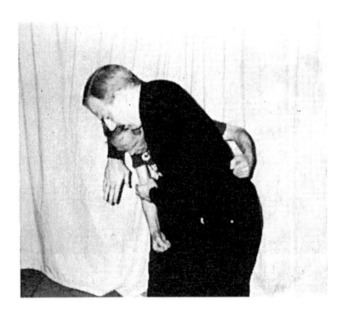

Another defense against a side headlock.

Defense: Immediately attack his groin and kidneys with punches and knuckle strikes.

Against a downward swing with a club.

Defense: Side step to your right; pivot on your right foot, swinging your left leg and body away from the blow. Keep your arms down. When the weapon misses you, step in on your right leg (keeping your right side toward him) and deliver a right hand chop to the bridge of his nose or his throat. Follow with a left front-kick to his groin.

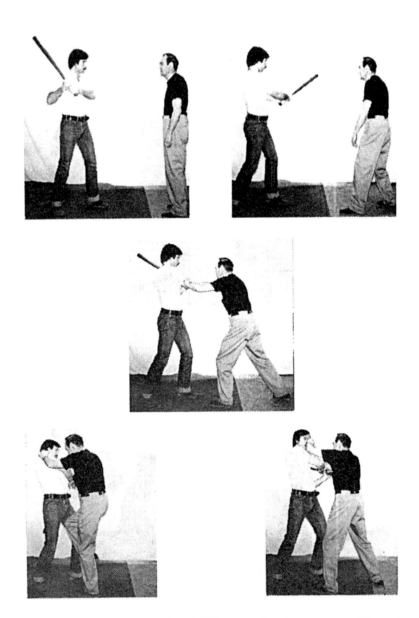

Attacker comes at you with a baseball bat or other long weapon. His posture indicates he will use a common baseball swing.

Defense: As the bat swings toward you, jump back quickly causing him to miss. Before he can start the back swing, rush in and pin his arm at the elbow and forearm with both hands. Chop to the bridge of nose or throat. Follow with knee to groin.

 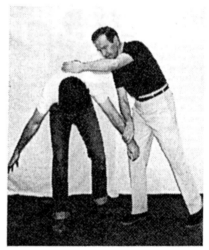

Attacker, with a hammer in his right hand, reaches for you with his left hand.

Defense: Stepping back on your left leg, grab his left wrist with your right hand and steer him out to his right side. Deliver a right side-kick to his leading (left) leg at the knee. Finish him off with a chop on the back of the neck.

Attacker comes up behind you and puts a club or stick across the front of your throat.

Defense: With your left hand, grab the weapon on your right side. Stepping forward on your left leg, drop your right shoulder and hit back with your right elbow. Deliver a right back-fist to his face. Take hold of the weapon and use it against him as shown.

Attacker puts a club or stick across the front of your neck from behind. This time you are sitting in a chair or park bench.

Defense: As in the standing attack, grab the weapon on the right side with your left hand. Pull forward and turn to your right to loosen the hold. Raise the weapon over your head hitting back with your elbow. As you stand, deliver a right back-fist blow to his face. Again, as in the standing attack, use the weapon on him.

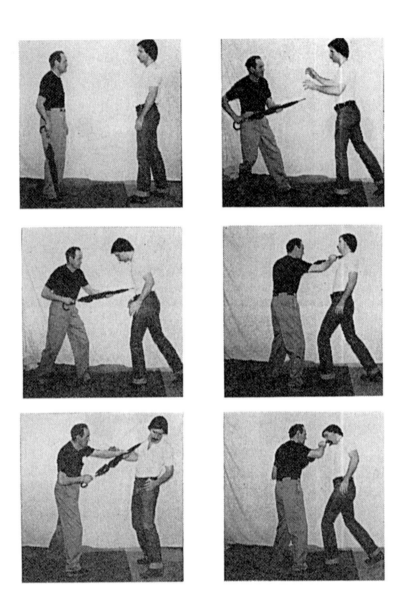

Using an umbrella (or stick) for defense:

With umbrella at your right side, step back on your right leg bringing your left hand up to grab umbrella as shown. In bayonet fighting this is called the "on guard" position.

Make a low thrust to the stomach. Stepping in, strike high to face, eyes, or throat. Turn sharply and jab face with the point. Follow up with the handle to the face or temple.

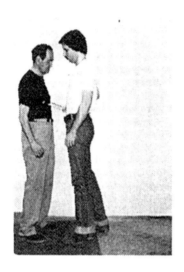 

Attacker holds a knife to your stomach.

Defense: As you step back on your right leg, push your attacker's knife hand away from you and toward him. Keep his knife hand pinned to his body and punch to the face. Your blow should knock him back far enough to allow you to deliver a right front-kick to his groin. Finish him off.

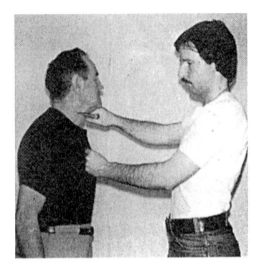 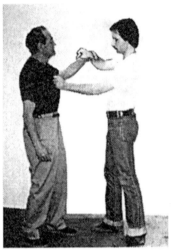

Attacker grabs you by the shirt with his left hand, and holds the blade of his knife across the front of your throat.

Defense: As you step back on your right leg, push your attacker's knife hand away from you and toward him. Immediately deliver a left front kick to his groin. When he bends forward, chop to the back of his neck. Remember to keep hold of his knife-hand!

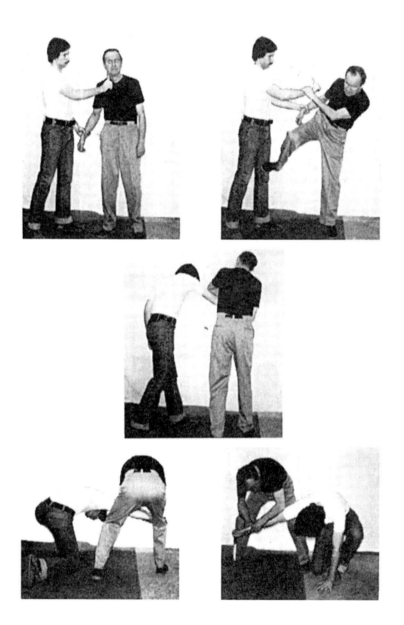

Attacker (on your right side) holds a knife against the right side of your neck.

Defense: Because you can see his right wrist, you can push it toward him and away from you. At the same time, deliver a right side-kick to his left knee. Finish him off with the arm lock shown.

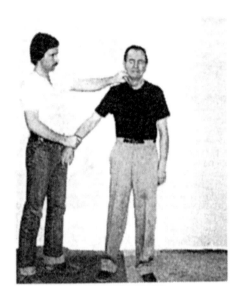

Attacker (on your right side) grabs your right wrist and holds a knife in his left hand against the right side of your neck.

Defense: Lean sharply away from the knife and deliver a right side-kick to his knee. Follow up appropriately.

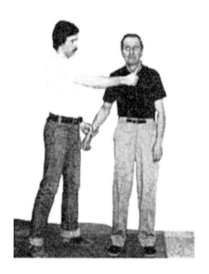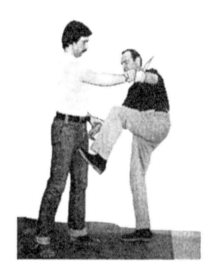

Attacker (on your right side) grabs your right wrist and holds a knife in his right hand against the left side of your neck.

Defense: Stepping back on your right leg away from the blade, turn to face your attacker. At the same time, deflect his knife-hand by grabbing with your left hand and holding at arm's length. Immediately deliver a front-kick to his groin. When he bends over, chop to the back of his neck at the base of the brain (medulla). Follow up with a knee to his face.

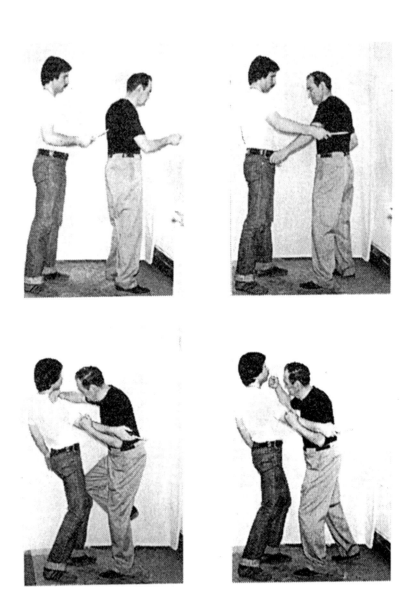

Attacker holds a knife (in his right hand) to your back as you are locking or unlocking a door.

Defense: Quickly turn to your left and wrap up his right arm as shown. Deliver a right hand punch to his face. Drive your right knee up into his groin. Should the knife be in his left hand, the defense is the same except for the follow-up. In that case, follow up with a right hand chop to his throat or the bridge of his nose.

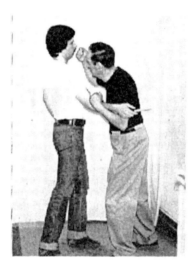

Attacker holds a knife to your back as you are locking or unlocking a door. This time he holds your left elbow.

Defense: Quickly turn to your left (his left will follow) and wrap up his right arm as shown. Deliver a right hand punch to his face. Follow up appropriately.

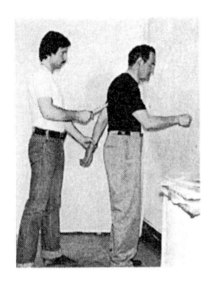 

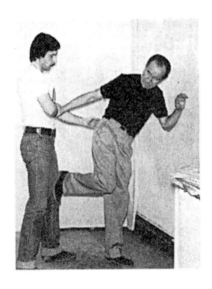 

Same attack - this time he holds your left wrist. This situation is more difficult.

Defense: Snap your left arm up and forward to break against his thumb. At the same time, deflect his right arm backwards. Keep his forearm pinned to his body as you back-kick to his knee. Follow up with a left to his face.

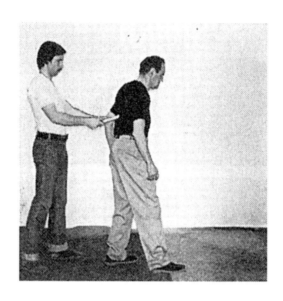

Attacker grabs your left elbow and puts a knife to your back. This time he tells you to keep walking.

Defense: Start walking forward, feigning compliance. When your right foot is forward, deliver a left back-kick to his leg just above the knee.

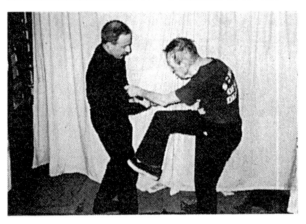

Attacker points gun at chest.

Defense: Grab gun (barrel or slide) with your left hand, deflecting it to your right. Simultaneously, side step to the left, pivoting your body off the line of fire. Using both hands, twist the gun so that it points toward the attacker. Attack his knee with kicks; keep attacking until he releases the weapon.

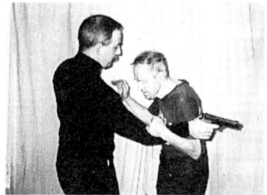

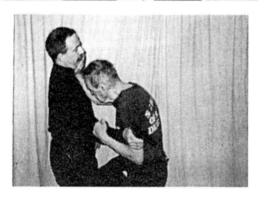

Attacker holds gun to back.

Defense: Quickly turn to your left and wrap up his right arm as shown. Attack with palm-heel blows to chin; thrust your right knee up into his groin. Should the gun be in his left hand, the wrap-up is similar; attack with right hand chop to his throat or the bridge of his nose. After softening up the attacker, reach over to grab gun and disarm.

 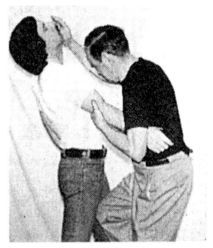

Attacker attempts to pistol-whip you—the gun is in his right hand.

Defense: Block with your left arm while swaying a bit to your right and stepping forward on your right leg. Wrap up his right arm as you step in on your left leg and deliver a right palm-heel thrust to his chin. Follow with a right knee to his groin.

Section III
The Gray Manual

DEFENSE

TECHNIQUES

By CHARLES NELSON

STREET TECHNIQUES
BY NEW YORK'S
"DIRTIEST" FIGHTER!

He may not look the part or carry "karate credentials" but people keep coming to him for his specialty: how to stay alive in the streets!

Recently a number of martial arts dojos have opened, claiming that their particular style is useful in a "street situation." Students are told that while they can perfect Oriental katas and learn their techniques, they will also be prepared to handle themselves in the event that they are accosted in the street.

Many people, especially those not familiar with the martial arts, feel that as long as a person knows karate or even judo, he will be more than capable of handling a stick-up or a mugging. However, there are some brown and black belts who fear they are less than qualified to take on a non-dojo situation. This is why they come to Charles Nelson.

Examples of martial artists who could not defend themselves outside their schools are legion. One Japanese black belt was held up at knifepoint in the hallway of his apartment building. He meekly gave the muggers what they wanted because he "didn't know what else to do."

Nelson operates a small school on the upper west side of Manhattan. His classes are small, and although he charges a fair amount of money for instruction, his students come away with techniques vital to their protection outside on the city streets.

Does the Nelson System of Self - Defense really work? Over the years a number of people have written in, describing incidents that would have been very dangerous had it not been for their study with Charley.

Nelson is glad that there had been a proliferation of interest in karate and other martial arts these days. Due to film "and television exploitation, Nelson feels that many people have taken an interest in karate because it became a fad. Now, however, he thinks that most people who study are genuinely interested in perfecting their skills.

In the final analysis, the best thing one can do when confronted by a mugger, says Nelson, is try to talk your way out of it. Sometimes the mere confidence a person projects helps him out of tight spots. Somehow the potential attacker recognizes that you are not afraid, and many times he is willing to look for an easier, victim.

No doubt there will be a number of people who feel that a man with no specific credentials shouldn't be training people in the martial arts. Nelson couldn't care less; he is interested in teaching people what works. And as far as he is concerned—if it works, use it.

Basic Defense Exercises

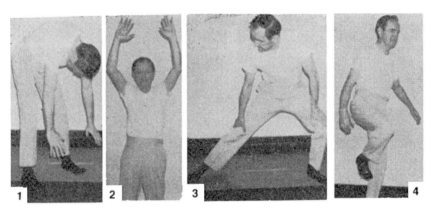

Simple practice exercises. Raise hands and touch your toes (1 & 2). Side stretch from left to right (3). Practice front kick so that it becomes automatic (4 & 5). Also side kicks with each foot (6). Practice jabbing with one hand and then the other (7 & 8).

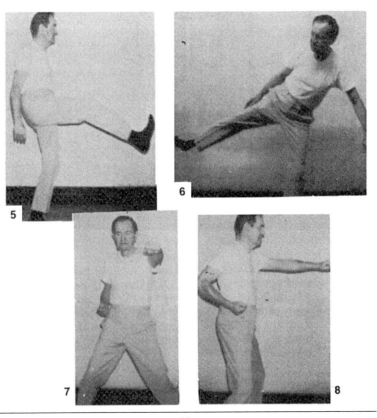

Defense Against Grabber with Knife

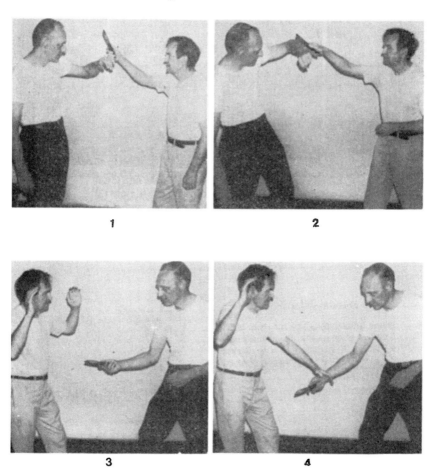

Never block with your left hand. Attacker can cut and even sever your arm. (1 & 2) The right way is to step back and raise both hands. (3) You are now ready to hit down on his right wrist. (4) Follow with a right hand punch to the jaw (5), and a kick to the groin (6). This should cripple attacker and leave him at your mercy.

5

6

Hands Off a Knife

Never grab knife with your bare hand. Attacker is on guard and can stash or thrust in any direction. (1 & 2) You are liable to receive badly cut or severed fingers. (3)

1

2

3

Defense Against Knife Attack

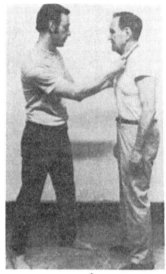 

1   2

Attacker grabs with left hand and holds knife against left side of your neck. (1) Side step to right, away from the blade. (2) At the same time deflect his wrist out to your left, holding on tightly with left hand. (3) Bring up point of left foot to his groin causing him to bend forward. Chop into base of brain to disable him. (4)

3   4

Defense Against Choker

1

2

When grabbed by the throat, (1) grasp attacker's left wrist with your right hand. (2) Step back on left leg, turning left, and pull him forward off balance to break his hold. Give a right side kick above the knee to damage or break the knee joint. (3) Change hands, continue forward pull and hit with right hand on back of the neck.

3

Defense Against Clothes Grabber

1   2

Opponent grabs your clothing with left hand, ready to push with his right. (1) Side step diagonally forward on your right foot, away from his pushing hand. At the same time, give a left hand heel thrust under the chin, (2) snapping his head back. Almost immediately, bring up left knee to his groin. (3) He will fall forward and you can chop at back of his neck. (4)

3   4

Defense Against Knife Held to Throat

1

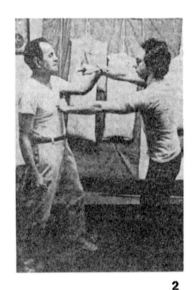

2

A major portion of instruction is devoted to dealing with various knife assaults. Always, the first rule of self-defense is to neutralize the knife, making it impossible for the attacker to use the weapon. As attacker holds the knife to Nelson's throat, (1) he takes a step back on his right foot and rolls his head back at the same time (2) to get out of the way of the knife. At the same time, he grabs the knife hand (3) pushing it

(continued)

3

4

toward the other man. The knife is now away from his throat and the other man's hand is useless. Quickly, he readies his knee for a kick to the groin (4) causing the other man to bend over. He then delivers a shuto to the base of the skull (5). As the man continues to fall, Nelson slips his arm in for a bar hammer lock (6) easily breaking the man's arm (7).

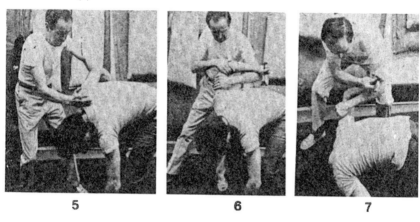

5   6   7

Defense Against the Lapel Grab

When someone steps in close with the intention of grabbing and possibly punching you, there is no time for fancy techniques. You've got to get the job done, and done quickly. As his attacker grabs him by the shirt front (1), Nelson quickly reaches up with both hands (2) and executes fingerstabs to the man's eyes (3). If he's wearing

(continued)

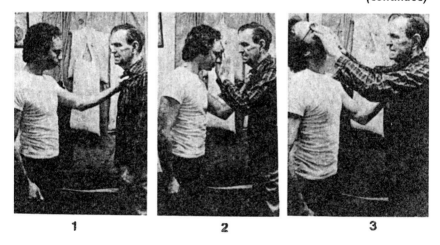

1   2   3

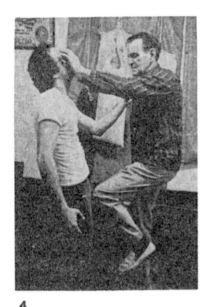

4

5

glasses, chances are you'll do even more damage to him than you anticipated. With his opponent blinded thus, Nelson proceeds to send a swift knee smash to his groin (4). That should double him over nicely (5) for the hard shuto that immediately follows (6). Once down (7), the man is at your mercy.

6

7

Defense Against Knife at Your Back

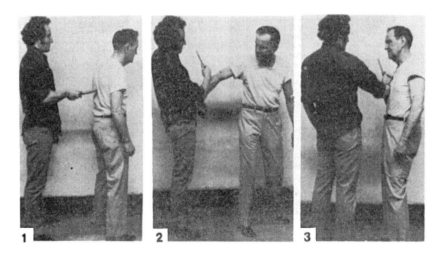

Attacker puts knife at your back. (1) Turn to your right, letting your right forearm push the knife hard towards his stomach. (2) Wrap up his right arm between your forearm and wrist. Bring your body in close to your right fist, trapping his arm between your right arm and chest. (3) Meantime give a chop to the throat with your left hand (4) and bring up your right knee to the groin. (5) Finish him off with a chop on the neck.

Defense Against Roundhouse Kick

1 **2**

Some karate buffs like to demonstrate their prowess. In the event that should happen, Nelson suggests the following strategy. As the man moves in with a leading left roundhouse kick (1) Nelson pulls his stomach and hips back to get out of the way (2). At the same time he uses a two-hand scooping block to catch the leg (3). With the leg caught, he moves down with a backfist to the groin (4) and a shuto to the kidneys (5 & 6). He now simply lifts the man's foot in the air, dumping him on the floor. This defense requires no real strength, only quickness.

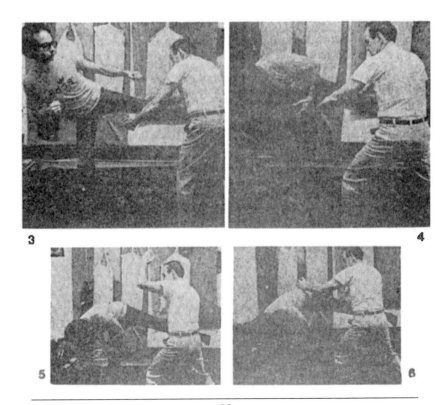

3 **4**

5 **6**

Defense Against Knife Slash

1

2

The natural instinct is to block a slashing knife with the same hand you would use if he were throwing a punch. Unfortunately, this has led to many a cut and mutilated arm. The trick is to use the other hand. This time Nelson becomes the attacker and moves in for a slash to the face (1). Sidestepping the knife, man moves to his right in a half circular motion, remembering to stay "inside" the blade. While he blocks with his right forearm (2) he locks his elbow joint. Immediately he grabs Nelson's wrist

(continued)

3

4

5

6

with his left hand, immobilizing the arm (3) Now that the knife is taken care of, he delivers a quick strike to the throat. (4) Grabbing Nelson's shoulder for balance, he delivers a kick to the groin, sending him to the ground. (5 & 6). A shuto to the back of the neck (7 & 8) and the attacker is put away for good.

7

8

Defense Against Low Knife Thrust

1

2

Again Nelson makes use of the bar hammer lock. As the man attempts to thrust into him (1) he pulls his stomach in and steps back and simultaneously blocks the other man's knife hand with his opposite hand (2). In one motion he now puts on the bar hammer lock by reaching for the man's elbow (3) rolling it forward to his right side (4) and

(continued)

3

4

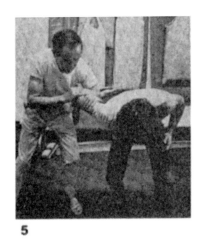

5

6

coming in with his left hand in the middle of the other man's upper arm between his elbow and shoulder (5). Pressing up with his right hand and down with his left (6) would simply snap the man's arm. A strike to the back of the neck (7 & 8) and down he goes (9).

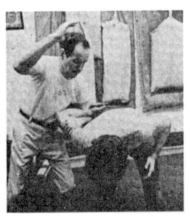

7

8

9

Defense Against a Mugging By Two Men

1 **2**

This is the typical mugging situation involving two attackers. Usually they try to mug the victim from the front and rear. From the rear, attacker holds a knife around Nelson's neck (1). Again, getting away from the knife is the main concern. Nelson moves his head into attacker's arm (2) using his right hand to grab knife hand. This pushes the knife outwards (3). As attacker moves in (4) Nelson gives him a kick to the groin (5 & 6) stunning him for the time being.

(continued)

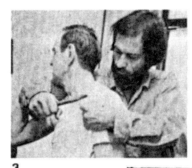

3 **4**

5

6   7

Now, he turns in towards the man with the knife (7) giving him an elbow strike to the solar plexus (8). Finally, he sends him down with a strike to the throat (9 & 10) and a knee to the groin (11 & 12). Making sure attacker does not rise to help his accomplice, Nelson applies a kick to the face (13).

8   9

10

11

12

13